Discover the Immeasurable

J. Krishnamurti

HOHM PRESS
Chino Valley, Arizona

Cover design: Adi Zuccarello, a.zuccarello@gmail.com
Interior design and layout: Zac Parker, zdpdigitalmedia@gmail.com

Library of Congress Cataloging-in-Publication Data

Krishnamurti, J. (Jiddu), 1895-1986.
[Talks. Selections]
Discover the immeasurable / J. Krishnamurti.
    pages cm
Six talks given in September 1956, taken from The Collected Works of J. Krishnamurti, Volume X of XVII.
ISBN 978-1-935387-56-5 (trade paper : alk. paper)
1. Spiritual life. I. Title.
B5134.K754A5 2014
181'.4--dc23
                            2013038804

Hohm Press
PO Box 4410
Chino Valley, AZ 86323
800-381-2700
www.hohmpress.com

CONTENTS

FIRST TALK

*Can you and I discover something
which is immeasurable?*

I think it is important to establish a right relationship between yourself and myself because you may be under the erroneous impression that I am going to talk about a complicated philosophy, or that I am bringing a particular system of philosophical thought from India, or that I have peculiar ideas which I want you to accept. So I think we should begin by establishing a relationship between us in which there is mutual understanding of each other.

I am not speaking as an Indian, nor do I believe that any particular philosophy or religion is going to solve our human problems. No human problem can be understood or resolved through a special way of thinking or through any dogma or belief. Though I happen to come from India, we have essentially the same problems there as you have here. We are human beings, not Germans or Hindus, English or Russians; we are human beings, living in a very complex society, with innumerable problems—economic, social, and above all, I think, religious. If we can understand the religious problem, then perhaps we shall be able to solve the contradictory national, economic, and social problems.

To understand the complex problem of religion, I think it is essential not to hold on to any particular idea or belief, but to listen with a mind that is not prejudiced so that we are capable of thinking out the problem together. Surely we must approach all our human problems with a very simple, direct clarity and understanding.

Our minds have been conditioned from childhood to think in a certain way; we are educated, brought up in a fixed pattern of thought. We are tradition bound. We have special values, certain opinions, and unquestioned beliefs, and according to this pattern we live—or at least we try to live. And I think therein lies the calamity. Because, life is in constant movement, is it not? It is a living thing, with extraordinary changes; it is never the same. And our problems also are never the same; they are ever changing. But we approach life with a mind that is fixed, opinionated; we have definite ideas and predetermined evaluations. So, for most of us, life becomes a series of complex and apparently insoluble problems, and invariably we turn to someone else to guide us, to help us, to show us the right path.

Here, I think, it would be right for me to point out that I am not doing anything of that kind. What we are going to do, if you are willing, is to think out the problem together. After all, it is your life, and to understand it, surely, you must understand yourself. The understanding of yourself does not depend on the sanctions of another.

So it seems to me that if we are at all serious, and if we would understand the many problems that exist in the world at the present time—the nationalism, the wars, the hatred, the racial divisions, and the divisions that the organized religions bring about—if we would understand all this and eliminate the conflict between man and man, it is imperative that we should first understand ourselves. Because, what we are, we project—which is a very simple fact. If I am nationalistic, I help to create a separative society— which is one of the seeds, the causes of war. So it is obviously essential that we understand ourselves, and this, it seems to me, is the major issue in our lives.

Religion is not to be found in a set of dogmas, beliefs, rituals; I think it is something much greater and far beyond all that. Therefore, it is imperative to understand why the mind clings to any particular religion or belief, to any particular dogma. It is only when we understand and free the mind from these beliefs, dogmas, and fears that there is a possibility of finding out if there is a reality, if there is God. But merely to believe, to follow, seems to me an utter folly.

So, if we are to understand each other, I think it is necessary for you to realize that I am not speaking to you as a group, as a number of Germans, but to each one as an individual human being, because the individual problem is the world problem. It is what we are as individuals that create society, society being the relationship between ourselves and others. I am speaking—and please believe it—as one individual to another, so that together we may understand the many problems that confront us. I am not establishing myself as an authority to tell you what to do because I do not believe in authority in spiritual matters. All authority is evil, and all sense of authority must cease, especially if we would find out what is God, what is truth, whether there is something beyond the mere measure of the mind. That is why it is very important for the individual to understand himself.

I know the inevitable question will arise: If we have no authority of any kind, will there not be anarchy? Of course there may be. But does authority create order? Or does it merely create a blind following that has no meaning at all except that it leads to destruction, to misery? But if we begin to understand ourselves—which is a very complex process— then we shall also begin to understand the anatomy of authority. Then I think we shall be able to find out, as individuals, what is true. Without the compulsion of society, without the authority of a religion or of any person, however great, without the influence of another, we shall be able to discover and experience for ourselves something beyond mere intellection, beyond the clever assertions of the mind.

So, I hope this much is very clear between us that I am not speaking as an Indian, with a particular philosophy, nor am I here to convince you of anything. I am asking, as one individual to another, whether it is possible to find out what is true, what is God—if there is God. It seems to me that one must begin by understanding oneself. And to understand yourself, surely, you must first know what you actually are, not what you think you should be—which is an ideological fallacy. After all, if I want to know myself, I must see myself exactly as I am, not as I think I ought to be. The "ought to be" is a form of illusion, an escape from what I am.

What we are concerned with—as individuals, not as a group—is to find out what is beyond the beliefs and theories, beyond the sentimental hopes and intellectual assertions of the various organized religions. We are trying to experience directly for ourselves if there is such a thing as reality, something more than the mere projections of the mind, which is what most religions are, however pleasant, however comforting. Can the mind find out, experience directly? Because direct experience alone has validity. Can you and I as individuals, by going into this question now, discover or experience something which is immeasurable? Because such an experience—if it is valid, if it is not just an illusion, a vision, a passing fantasy—has an extraordinary significance in life. Such an experience transforms one's life and brings about a morality that is not mere social respectability.

So, is it possible for you who are listening to me to experience that which is immeasurable? Just to say yes or no would be an absurdity. All that we can do is to find out if the mind is capable of experiencing something which is not a projection of its own demands. Which means, really, can you, the individual, free yourself from all your conditioning? Can you cease completely to be the Christian who believes, who has certain formulas, certain ideals? After all, each one is brought up in a particular tradition, and his God is the God of that tradition. Surely, that is not reality; it is merely a repetition of what he has been told. To find out if there is a reality, one must free oneself from the tradition in which one has been brought up—and that is an extraordinarily difficult thing to do. But only then is it possible to go beyond the mere measure of the mind and experience something which is immeasurable. If we do not experience that, life is very empty, trivial, lonely, without much meaning.

How is one, being serious and earnest, to set about it? Because without the fragrance, without the perfume of that reality, life is very shallow, materialistic, miserable; there is constant tension, striving, ceaseless pain and suffering. So a serious person must surely ask himself this question: Is it possible to experience something which is not a mere wish or intellectual concept from which one derives a certain satisfaction but something entirely new, beyond the fabrications of the mind? And if it is possible, then what is one to do? How is one to set about it?

I think there is only one approach to this problem, which is to see that until I know myself, until I know the whole content of the mind, the unconscious as well as the conscious, with all its intricate workings—until I am cognizant of all that, fully aware of it, I cannot possibly go beyond. Can I know myself in this way? Can I know myself as a whole—all the motives, the urges, the compulsions, the fears—and not just a few reactions and responses of the conscious mind? And can anyone help me, or must this be done entirely by myself? Because if I look to another for help, I become dependent, which means that the other becomes my authority; and when I only know myself through the authority of another, I do not know myself at all. And merely reading psychological books is of very little importance because I can only know myself as I am by observing my living from day to day, watching myself in the mirror of my relationship with another. To watch myself in that mirror is not to be merely introspective or objective, but to be constantly alert, watchful of what is taking place in the mind, in myself.

You will find that it is extraordinarily difficult to watch yourself in the mirror of relationship without any sense of condemning what you see, and if you condemn what you see, you do not understand it. To understand a thing as it is, condemnation, judgment, evaluation must go, which is extremely difficult because at present we are trained, educated to condemn, to reject, to approve, to deny.

And that is only the beginning of it, a very shallow beginning. But one must go through that, one must understand the whole process of the mind, not merely intellectually, verbally, but as one lives from day to day, watching oneself in this mirror of relationship. One must actually experience what is taking place in the mind—examine it, be aware of the whole content of it, without denying, suppressing, or putting it away. Then, if you go so far, and if you are at all serious, you will find that the mind is no longer projecting any image, no longer creating any myth, any illusion; it is beginning to understand the totality of itself, and therefore it becomes very clear, simple, quiet.

This is not a momentary process but a continual living, a continual sharpening of the mind. And in the very process of sharpening, the mind spontaneously ceases to be as it is. Then the mind is no longer creating images, visions, fallacies, illusions; and only then, when the mind is completely still, silent, is there a possibility of experiencing something which is not of the mind itself. But this requires not just one day of effort, or a casual observation, or attending one talk, but a slow maturity, a deepening search, a greater, wider, totally integrated outlook, so that the mind which is now driven by many influences and demands, inhibited by so many fears is free to inquire, to experience.

Only such a mind is truly religious—not the mind that believes or disbelieves in God, that has innumerable beliefs, that joins, agrees, follows, or denies; such a mind can never find out what is truth. That is why it is very important for those who are serious, for those who are concerned with the welfare of mankind, to put aside all their vain beliefs and theories, all their associations with particular religious organizations, and inquire very deeply within themselves.

For after all, religion is not dogma, it has nothing to do with belief; religion does not mean going to church or performing certain rituals. None of that is religion; it is merely the invention of man to control man. And if one would find out whether there is a reality, something beyond the inventions of the mind, one must put aside all these absurdities, this childish thinking. It is very difficult for most people to put it all aside because in clinging to beliefs, they feel secure; it gives them some hope. But to discover reality, to experience something beyond the mind, the mind must cease to have any form of security. It must be totally denuded of all refuges. It is only such a mind that is purified, and then it is possible for the mind to experience something which is beyond itself.

I have been given some questions, and I shall try to answer some of them—or rather, together we shall try to unravel the problem. There is no one answer to a problem, there is no isolated solution. If we merely look for a solution to a problem, we shall find that our search for the solution creates other problems. Whereas, if we are capable of examining the problem itself, without trying to find an answer, we shall discover that the answer is in the problem. So it is very important to know how to approach the problem. The mind which has a problem and seeks an answer, cannot possibly inquire into the problem itself because it is concerned only with the solution. To understand any problem, you must give your whole attention to it, and you cannot give your whole attention to it if you are seeking a solution, an answer.

Question: We are full of memories of the last war, with all its terror. Can we ever free our minds of the past and start anew?

KRISHNAMURTI: The problem of memory is very complex, is it not? We have pleasant memories and unpleasant memories. We want to reject the unpleasant, the terrible, the painful memories, and keep the pleasant ones. That is what we are always trying to do, is it not? The pleasant memories of our youth, the interesting things we have read, the stimulating experiences we have had—all this has significance for us, and we want to hold on to it; but the things which are painful, sorrowful, unpleasant, irritating, we reject. So we divide our memories into the pleasant and the unpleasant, and what we are mostly concerned with is how to put away the unpleasant memories and keep alive those that are pleasant. But so long as we divide memory into the pleasant and the unpleasant and try to get rid of the unpleasant, there will always be conflict, both within and without.

I do not know if I am making myself clear. The mind is full of memories, it is made up of memories. You have no mind without memory—the memories of your past, of all the things you have learned, experienced, lived, suffered. Mind is memory, conscious or unconscious. In memory there is the pleasant and the unpleasant, and we want to reject the unpleasant; we want to keep the desirable and get rid of the undesirable, so there is always a conflict going on. What we have to understand is not how to retain the pleasant and be free of the terrible memories, but rather how to eliminate the desire to keep some memories and reject others, which creates conflict. What is important is to be aware of this conflict, and to understand why it is that the mind gathers memories and holds on to them.

Obviously one needs certain memories in order to live in this world. I must remember how to get back to the place where I live, and so on. But such memories are no problem to us. For most of us the problem is how to get rid of the memories which are painful, destructive, while retaining those which are significant, purposeful, enjoyable. But why does the mind cling to the one and seek to reject the other? Please follow this. If you do not hold fast to the pleasant memories, what are you? If you had no memories of the pleasant, of the hopeful, of the enjoyable, of the things that you have lived for, you would feel nonhuman, you would feel lost, a nobody. The mind clings to its pleasant memories because without them it would be lonely, in despair.

So I do not think the problem is how to get rid of the unpleasant memories, the terrors of the past. That is fairly easy. If you deliberately set about to wipe out the past, it can be done comparatively simply. But what is much more complex, what demands much deeper thought and inquiry, is to go into the whole problem of memory—not only the conscious memories, but the deep, underlying memories which guide our lives.

After all, a memory much deeper than the memory of the war and all the bestiality of it is that which makes you call yourself a German or a Christian or a Hindu; that also is part of memory, is it not? And that gives you solidarity, it gives you companionship, it makes you feel equal or superior to others, it gives you a sense of courage, and so many other things. But must you not also be free of that memory? Must one not be free to inquire, to go much further than the mere reaction to memories, which is a process of living in the past?

You see, memory does not yield to the newness of life. Memory is only the past, and anything born of memory is always old, never new. To discover something totally new, the mind must be astonishingly quiet, still, not active, not desiring and reacting to memories.

Question: We have had enough of war. We want peace. How can we prevent a new war?

KRISHNAMURTI: I do not think there is a simple answer because the causes of war are many. So long as there is nationalism, so long as you are a German or a Russian or an American, clinging to sovereignty, to an exclusive nationality, you are sure to have war.

So long as you are a Christian and I am a Hindu, or you are a Muslim and I am a Buddhist, there is bound to be war. So long as you are ambitious, wanting to reach the top of your society, seeking achievement and worshiping success, you will be a cause of war.

But we are brought up on all this. We are trained to compete, to succeed, to be ambitious, to serve a particular government, to belong to a particular country or religion. Our whole education cultivates the competitive spirit and guides the mind towards war. And can we, as individual human beings, change all this? Can you and I individually cease to be ambitious, cease to regard ourselves as Germans or Indians, cease to belong to any particular religion, to any particular group or ideology—communist, socialist, or any other—and be concerned only with human welfare?

So long as we remain attached to a group or to an ideology, so long as we are ambitious, seeking success, we are bound to create war. It may not be a war of outward destruction, but we will have conflict between each other and within ourselves, which is actually a form of war. I do not think we see this, and even if we do, we are not serious about it. We want some miraculous event to take place to stop war, while we continue to live as we are in the present social structure, making money, seeking position, power, prestige, trying to become famous, and all the rest of it. That is our pattern, and so long as that pattern exists in our minds and hearts, we are bound to produce war.

After all, war is merely the catastrophic effect of our daily living, and so long as we do not change our daily living, no amount of legislation, controls, and sanctions will prevent war. Is peace in the mind and heart, in the way of our life, or is it merely a governmental regulation, something to be decided in the United Nations? I am afraid that for most of us, peace is only a matter of legislation, and we are not concerned with peace in our own minds and hearts; therefore, there can be no peace in the world. You cannot have peace, inward or outward, so long as you are ambitious, competitive, so long as you regard yourself as a German, a Hindu, a Russian, or an Englishman, so long as you are striving to become somebody in this mad world. Peace comes only when you understand all this and are no longer pursuing success in a society which is already corrupt. Only the peaceful mind, the mind that understands itself, can bring peace in the world.

September 5, 1956

SECOND TALK

*Is it possible to forget oneself
without any motive?*

I think it is important, in listening to each other, to find out
for oneself if what is being said is true; that is, to experience
it directly and not merely argue about whether what is said
is true or false, which would be completely useless. And
perhaps this evening we can find out if it is possible to set
about the very complex process of forgetting oneself.

Many of us must have experienced, at one time or
another, that state when the "me," the self, with its
aggressive demands, has completely ceased, and the mind
is extraordinarily quiet, without any direct volition—that
state wherein, perhaps, one may experience something
that is without measure, something that it is impossible to
put into words. There must have been these rare moments
when the self, the "me," with all its memories and travails,
with all its anxieties and fears, has completely ceased.
One is then a being without any motive, without any
compulsion, and in that state one feels or is aware of an

astonishing sense of immeasurable distance, of limitless space and being.

This must have happened to many of us. And I think it would be worthwhile if we could go into this question together and see whether it is possible to resolve the enclosing, limiting self, this restricting "me" that worries, that has anxieties, fears, that is dominating and dominated, that has innumerable memories, that is cultivating virtue and trying in every way to become something, to be important. I do not know if you have noticed the constant effort that one is consciously or unconsciously making to express oneself, to be something, either socially, morally, or economically. This entails, does it not, a great deal of striving; our whole life is based on the everlasting struggle to arrive, to achieve, to become. The more we struggle, the more significant and exaggerated the self becomes, with all its limitations, fears, ambitions, frustrations; and there must have been times when each one has asked himself whether it is not possible to be totally without the self.

After all, we do have rare moments when the sense of the self is not. I am not talking of the transmutation of the self to a higher level, but of the simple cessation of the "me" with its anxieties, worries, fears—the absence of the self. One realizes that such a thing is possible, and then one sets about deliberately, consciously, to eliminate the self. After all, that is what organized religions try to do—to help each worshiper, each believer, to lose himself in something greater, and thereby perhaps to experience some higher state. If you are not a so-called religious person, then you identify yourself with the state, with the country, and try to lose yourself in that identification, which gives you the feeling of greatness, of being something much larger than the petty, little self, and all the rest of it. Or, if we do not do that, we try to lose ourselves in social work of some kind, again with the same intention. We think that if we can forget ourselves, deny ourselves, put ourselves out of the way by dedicating our lives to something much greater and more vital than ourselves, we shall perhaps experience a bliss, a happiness, which is not merely a physical sensation. And if we do none of these things, we hope to stop thinking about ourselves through the cultivation of virtue, through discipline, through control, through constant practice.

Now, I do not know if you have thought about it, but all this implies, surely, a ceaseless effort to be or become something. And perhaps in listening to what is being said, we can together go into the whole process and discover for ourselves whether it is possible to wipe away the sense of the "me" without this fearful, restricting discipline, without this enormous effort to deny ourselves, this constant struggle to renounce our wants, our ambitions, in order to be something or to achieve some reality. I think in this lies the real issue.

Because all effort implies motive, does it not? I make an effort to forget myself in something, in some ritual or ideology, because in thinking about myself, I am unhappy. When I think about something else, I am more relaxed, my mind is quieter, I seem to feel better, I look at things differently. So I make an effort to forget myself. But behind my effort there is a motive, which is to escape from myself because I suffer, and that motive is essentially a part of the self. When I renounce this world and become a monk or a very devout religious person, the motive is that I want to achieve something better, but that is still the process of the self, is it not? I may give up my name and just be a number in a religious order, but the motive is still there.

Now, is it possible to forget oneself without any motive? Because, we can see very well that any motive has within it the seed of the self with its anxiety, ambition, frustration, its fear of not-being, and the immense urge to be secure. And can all that fall away easily, without any effort? Which means, really, can you and I, as individuals, live in this world without being identified with anything? After all, I identify myself with my country, with my religion, with my family, with my name, because without identification, I am nothing. Without a position, without power, without prestige of one kind or another, I feel lost; and so I identify myself with my name, with my family, with my religion, I join some organization or become a monk—we all know the various types of identification that the mind clings to. But can we live in this world without any identification at all?

If we can think about this, if we can listen to what is being said, and at the same time be aware of our own intimations regarding the implications of identification, then I think we shall discover, if we are at all serious, that it is possible to live in this world without the nightmare of identification and the ceaseless struggle to achieve a result. Then, I think, knowledge has quite a different significance. At present we identify ourselves with our knowledge and use it as a means of self-expansion, just as we do with the nation, with a religion, or with some activity. Identification with the knowledge we have gained is another way of furthering the self, is it not? Through knowledge the "me" continues its struggle to be something, and thereby perpetuates misery, pain.

If we can very humbly and simply see the implications of all this, be aware, without assuming anything, of how our minds operate and what our thinking is based on, then I think we shall realize the extraordinary contradiction that exists in this whole process of identification. After all, it is because I feel empty, lonely, miserable, that I identify myself with my country, and this identification gives me a sense of well being, a feeling of power. Or, for the same reason, I identify myself with a hero, with a saint.

But if I can go into this process of identification very deeply, then I will see that the whole movement of my thinking and all my activity, however noble, is essentially based on the continuance of myself, in one form or another.

Now, if I once see that, if I realize it, feel it with my whole being, then religion has quite a different meaning. Then religion is no longer a process of identifying myself with God, but rather the coming into being of a state in which there is only that reality, and not the "me." But this cannot be a mere verbal assertion; it is not just a phrase to be repeated.

That is why it is very important, it seems to me, to have self-knowledge, which means going very deeply into oneself without assuming anything, so that the mind has no deceptions, no illusions, so that it does not trick itself into visions and false states. Then, perhaps, it is possible for the enclosing process of the self to come to an end—but not through any form of compulsion or discipline, because the more you discipline the self, the stronger the self becomes. What is important is to go into all this very deeply and patiently, without taking anything for granted, so that one begins to understand the ways, the purposes, the motives and directions of the mind. Then, I think, the mind comes to a state in which there is no identification at all, and therefore no effort to be something; then there is the cessation of the self, and I think that is the real.

Although we may swiftly, fleetingly experience this state, the difficulty for most of us is that the mind clings to the experience and wants more of it, and the very wanting of more is again the beginning of the self. That is why it is very important, for those of us who are really serious in these matters, to be inwardly aware of the process of our own thinking, to silently observe our motives, our emotional reactions, and not merely say, "I know myself very well"—for actually one does not. You may know your reactions and motives superficially, at the conscious level. But the self, the "me," is a very complex affair, and to go into the totality of the self needs persistent and continuous inquiry without a motive, without an end in view, and such inquiry is surely a form of meditation.

That immense reality cannot be found through any organization, through any church, through any book, through any person or teacher. One has to find it for oneself—which means that one has to be completely alone, uninfluenced. But we are, all of us, the result of so many influences, so many pressures, known and unknown; and that is why it is very important to understand these many pressures, influences, and be dissociated from them all so that the mind becomes extraordinarily simple, clear. Then, perhaps, it will be possible to experience that which cannot be put into words.

Question: You said yesterday that authority is evil. Why is it evil?

KRISHNAMURTI: Is not all "following" evil? Why do we follow authority of any kind? Why do we establish authority? Why do human beings accept authority—governmental, religious, every form of authority?

Authority does not come into being by itself; we create it. We create the tyrannical ruler, as well as the tyrannical priest with his gods, rituals, and beliefs. Why? Why do we create authority and become followers? Obviously, because we all want to be secure, we want to be powerful in different ways and in varying degrees. All of us are seeking position, prestige, which the leader, the country, the government, the minister, is offering—so we follow. Or we create the image of authority in our own minds and follow that image. The church is as tyrannical as the political leaders, and while we object to the tyranny of governments, most of us submit to the tyranny of the church or of some religious teacher.

If we begin to examine the whole process of following, we will see, I think, that we follow, first of all, because we are confused, and we want somebody to tell us what to do. And being confused, we are bound to follow those who are also confused, however much they may assert that they are the messengers of God or the saviors of the state. We follow because we are confused, and as we choose leaders, both religious and political, out of our confusion, we inevitably create more confusion, more conflict, more misery.

That is why it is very important for us to understand the confusion in ourselves, and not look to another to help us to clear it up. For how can a man who is confused know what is wrong and choose what is right, what is true? First he must clear up his own confusion. And once he has cleared up his own confusion, there is no choice; he will not follow anybody.

So we follow because we want to be secure, whether economically, socially, or religiously. After all, the mind is always seeking security; it wants to be safe in this world and also in the next world. All we are concerned with is to be secure, both with mammon and with God. That is why we create the authority of the government, the dictator, and the authority of the church, the idol, the image. So long as we follow, we must create authority, and that authority becomes ultimately evil because we have thoughtlessly given ourselves over to domination by another.

I think it is important to go deeply into this whole question and begin to understand why the mind insists on following. You follow, not only political and religious leaders, but also what you read in the newspapers, in magazines, in books; you seek the authority of the specialists, the authority of the written word. All this indicates, does it not, that the mind is uncertain of itself. One is afraid to think apart from what has been said by the leaders because one might lose one's job, be ostracized, excommunicated, or put into a concentration camp. We submit to authority because all of us have this inward demand to be safe, this urge to be secure. So long as we want to be secure—in our possessions, in our power, in our thoughts—we must have authority, we must be followers; and in that lies the seed of evil, for it invariably leads to the exploitation of man by man. He who would really find out what truth is, what God is, can have no authority, whether of the book, of the government, of the image, or of the priest; he must be totally free of all that.

This is very difficult for most of us because it means being insecure, standing completely alone, searching, groping, never being satisfied, never seeking success. But if we seriously experiment with it, then I think we shall find that there is no longer any question of creating or following authority because something else begins to operate—which is not a mere verbal statement but an actual fact. The man who is ceaselessly questioning, who has no authority, who does not follow any tradition, any book or teacher, becomes a light unto himself.

Question: Why do you put so much emphasis on self-knowledge? We know very well what we are.

KRISHNAMURTI: I wonder if we do know what we are? We are, surely, everything that we have been taught; we are the totality of our past; we are a bundle of memories, are we not? When you say, "I belong to God," or "The self is eternal," and all the rest of it—that is all part of your background, your conditioning. Similarly, when the communist says, "There is no God," he also is reflecting his conditioning.

Merely to say, "Yes, I know myself very well," is just a superficial remark. But to realize, to actually experience that your whole being is nothing but a bundle of memories, that all your thinking, your reactions, are mechanical, is not at all easy. It means being aware not only of the workings of the conscious mind but also of the unconscious residue, the racial impressions, memories, the things that we have learned; it means discovering the whole field of the mind, the hidden as well as the visible, and that is extremely arduous. And if my mind is merely the residue of the past, if it is only a bundle of memories, impressions, shaped by so-called education and various other influences, then is there any part of me which is not all that? Because, if I am merely a repeating machine, as most of us are—repeating what we have learned, what we have gathered, passing on what has been told to us—then any thought arising within this conditioned field obviously can only lead to further conditioning, further misery and limitation.

So, can the mind, knowing its limitations, being aware of its conditioning, go beyond itself? That is the problem. Merely to assert that it *can* or it *cannot*, would be silly. Surely it is fairly obvious that the whole mind is conditioned. We are all conditioned—by tradition, by family, by experience, through the process of time. If you believe in God, that belief is the outcome of a particular conditioning, just as is the disbelief of the man who says he does not believe in God. So belief and disbelief have very little importance. But what is important is to understand the whole field of thought, and to see if the mind can go beyond it all.

To go beyond, you must know yourself. The motives, the urges, the responses, the immense pressure of what people have taught you, the dreams, the inhibitions, the conscious and hidden compulsions—you must know them all. Only then, I think, is it possible to find out if the mind, which is now so mechanical, can discover something totally new, something that has never been corrupted by time.

Question: You say that true religion is neither belief nor dogma nor ceremonies. What then is true religion?

KRISHNAMURTI: How are you going to find out? It is not for me just to answer, surely. How is the individual to find out what is true religion? We know what is generally called religion—dogma, belief, ceremonies, meditation, the practice of yoga, fasting, disciplining oneself, and so on. We all know the whole gamut of the so-called religious approach. But is that religion? And if I want to find out what is true religion, how am I to set about it?

First of all, I must obviously be free from all dogmas, must I not? And that is extraordinarily difficult. I may be free from the dogmas imposed upon me in childhood, but I may have created a dogma or belief of my own— which is equally pernicious. So, I must also be free from that. And I can be free only when I have no motive, when there is no desire at all to be secure, either with God or in this world. Again, this is extremely difficult because surreptitiously, deep down, the mind is always wanting a position of certainty. And there are all the images that have been imposed upon the mind, the saviors, the teachers, the doctrines, the superstitions—I must be free of all that. Then, perhaps, I shall find out what it is to be truly religious—which may be the greatest revolution, and I think it is. The only true revolution is not the economic revolution or the revolution of the communists, but the deep religious revolution that comes about when the mind is no longer seeking shelter in any dogma or belief, in any church or savior, in any teacher or sacred book. And I think such a revolution has immense significance in the world, for then the mind has no ideology, it is neither of the West nor of the East. Surely, this religious revolution is the only salvation.

To find out what is true religion requires, not a mere one-day effort or one-day search and forgetfulness the next day, but constant questioning, a disturbing inquiry, so that you begin to discard everything. After all, this process of discarding is the highest form of thinking. The pursuit of positive thinking is not thinking at all; it is merely copying. But when there is inquiry without a motive, without a desire for a result, which is the negative approach—in that inquiry the mind goes beyond all traditional religions; and then, perhaps, one may find out for oneself what God is, what truth is.

September 6, 1956

THIRD TALK

*Do ideals help to bring about
a radical change in us?*

I do not think that we realize the significance or the importance of the individual. Because, as I was saying the other day, to bring about a fundamental, religious revolution, one must surely cease to think in terms of the universal, in terms of the collective. Anything that is made universal, collective, belonging to everybody, can never be true—true in the sense of being directly experienced by each individual, uninfluenced, without the impetus of self-centered interest. I think we do not sufficiently realize the seriousness of this. Anything really true must be totally individual—not in the sense of self-centeredness, which is very limiting and which in itself is evil, but individual in the sense that each one of us must experience for himself, uninfluenced, something which is not the outcome of any self-centered interest or drive.

One can see in the modern world how everything is tending towards collective thought—everybody thinking alike. The various governments, though they do not compel it, are quietly and sedulously working at it. Organized religions are obviously controlling and shaping the minds of people according to their respective patterns, hoping thereby to bring about a universal morality, a universal experience. But I think that whatever is made universal in that sense, is always suspect because it can never be true; it has lost its vitality, its directness, its truth. Yet throughout the world we see this tendency to shape and to control the mind of man. And it is extraordinarily difficult to free the mind from this false universality and to change oneself without any self-interest.

It seems to me that we must have a change—a fundamental, radical change in our thinking, in our feeling. To bring about change, we use various methods; we have ideals, disciplines, sanctions, or we look to social, economic, and scientific influences. These things do bring about a superficial change, but I am not talking of that. I am talking of a change which is uninfluenced, without any self-interest, without self-centeredness. It seems to me that such a change is possible, and that it must come about if we are to have this religious revolution of which I was speaking the other day.

We think that ideals are necessary. But do ideals help to bring about this radical change in us? Or do they merely enable us to postpone, to push change into the future and thereby avoid the immediate, radical change? Surely, so long as we have ideals, we never really change but hold on to our ideals as a means of postponement, of avoiding the immediate change which is so essential. I know it is taken for granted by the majority of us that ideals are indispensable, for without them we think there would be no impetus to change, and we would rot, stagnate. But I am questioning whether ideals of any kind ever do transform our thinking.

Why do we have ideals? If I am violent, need I have the ideal of nonviolence? I do not know if you have thought about this at all. If I am violent—as most of us are in different degrees—is it necessary for me to have the ideal of nonviolence? Will the pursuit of nonviolence free the mind from violence? Or is the very pursuit of nonviolence actually an impediment to the understanding of violence? After all, I can understand violence only when, with my whole mind, I give complete attention to the problem. And the moment I am wholly concerned with violence and the understanding of violence, what significance has the ideal of nonviolence? It seems to me that the pursuit of the ideal is an evasion, a postponement. If I am to understand violence, I must give my whole mind to it and not allow myself to be distracted by the ideal of nonviolence.

This is really a very important issue. Most of us look upon the ideal as essential in order to make us change. But I think it is possible to bring about a change only when the mind understands the whole problem of violence, and to understand violence, you must give your complete attention to it, and not be distracted by an ideal.

We all see the importance of the cessation of violence. And how am I, as an individual, to be free of violence—not just superficially, but totally, completely, inwardly? If the ideal of nonviolence will not free the mind from violence, then will the analysis of the cause of violence help to dissolve violence?

After all, this is one of our major problems, is it not? The whole world is caught up in violence, in wars; the very structure of our acquisitive society is essentially violent. And if you and I as individuals are to be free from violence—totally, inwardly free, not merely superficially or verbally—then how is one to set about it without becoming self-centered?

You understand the problem, do you not? If my concern is to free the mind from violence, and I practice discipline in order to control violence and change it into nonviolence, surely that brings about self-centered thought and activity because my mind is focused all the time on getting rid of one thing and acquiring something else. And yet I see the importance of the mind being totally free from violence. So what am I to do? Surely, it is not a question of how one is not to be violent. The fact is that we are violent, and to ask, "How am I not to be violent?" merely creates the ideal, which seems to me to be utterly futile. But if one is capable of looking at violence and understanding it, then perhaps there is a possibility of resolving it totally.

So, how are we to resolve violence without becoming self-centered, without the "me" being completely occupied with itself and its problems? I do not know if you have thought about this matter. Most of us, I think, have accepted the easy path of pursuing the ideal of nonviolence. But if one is really concerned, deeply, inwardly, with how to resolve violence, then it seems to me that one must find out whether ideals are essential, and whether discipline, practice, the constant reminding of oneself not to be violent, can ever resolve violence or will merely exaggerate self-centeredness under the new name of nonviolence.

Surely, to discipline the mind towards the ideal of non-violence is still a self-centered activity and therefore only another form of violence.

If the problem is clear, then perhaps we can proceed to inquire into whether it is possible to free the mind from violence without being self-centered. This is very important, and I think it would be worthwhile if we could go into it hesitantly and tentatively and really find out. I see that any form of discipline, suppression, any effort to substitute an ideal for the fact—even though it be the ideal of love, or peace—is essentially a self-centered process, and that inherent in that process is the seed of violence. The man who practices nonviolence is essentially self-centered and therefore essentially violent because he is concerned about himself. To practice humility is never to be humble because the self-conscious process of acquiring humility, or cultivating any other virtue, is only another form of self-centeredness, which is inherently evil and violent. If I see this very clearly, then what am I to do? How am I to set about to free the mind from violence?

I do not know if you have thought about the problem at all in this manner. Perhaps this is the first time you have considered it, and so you may be inclined to say, "What nonsense!" But I do not think it is nonsense. After all, most idealists are very self-centered people because they are concerned with achievement. So the question is: Is it possible to free the mind from violence without the self-centered influence and activity? I think it is possible. But to really find out, one must inquire into it, not as part of a group, or the collective, but as an individual. As part of the collective, you have already accepted the ideal, and you practice virtue. But surely one must dissociate oneself totally from that whole process and inquire directly for oneself.

To inquire directly, one must ask oneself if the entity, the person who wants to get rid of violence, is different from the violence itself. When one acknowledges, "I am violent," is the "I" who then wishes to get rid of violence different from the quality which he calls violence? This may all sound a bit complicated, but if one will go into it patiently, I think one will understand without too much difficulty.

When I say, "I am violent," and wish to free myself from violence, is the entity who is violent different from the quality which he calls violence? That is, is the experiencer who feels he is violent different from the experience itself? Surely the experiencer is the same as the experience; he is not different or apart from the experience. I think this is very important to understand because if one really understood it, then in freeing the mind from violence, there would be no self-centered activity at all.

We have separated the thinker from the thought, have we not? We say, "I am violent, and I must make an effort to get rid of violence." In order to get rid of violence, we discipline ourselves, we practice nonviolence, we think about it every day and try to do something about it—which means we take it for granted that the "I," the maker of effort, is different from the experience, from the quality. But is this so? Are the two states different, or are they really a unit, one and the same?

Obviously, there is no thinker if there is no thought. But the thinker, the "I," who is the maker of effort, is always exercising his volition in getting rid of violence, so he has separated himself from the quality which he calls violence. But they are not separate, are they? They are a unity. And actually to experience that unitary state—which means not differentiating between the thinker and his thought, between the "I" who is violent and the violence itself—is essential if the mind is to be free from violence without self-centered action.

If you will think about it a little, I am sure you will see the truth of what I am trying to say. After all, just as the quality of the diamond cannot be separated from the diamond, so the quality of the thinker cannot be separated from thought itself. But we have separated them. In us there is ever the observer, the watcher, the censor, who is condemning, justifying, accepting, denying, and so on; the censor is always exercising influence on his thought. But the thought is the censor; the two are not separate, and it is essential to experience this in order to bring about a revolutionary change in which there is no self-centered activity.

After all, it is urgent that we change. We have had so many wars, such destruction, violence, terror, misery, and if we do not change radically, we shall go on pursuing the same old path. To change radically and not merely accept a new set of slogans, or give ourselves over to the state or to the church, to really understand the fundamental revolution that must take place in order to put an end to all this misery, it seems to me essential to discover whether there can be an action which is not self-centered. Surely, action will ever be self-centered as long as we do not experience directly for ourselves the fact that there is only thought and not the thinker. But if once we do experience this, I think we will find that effort then has quite a different significance.

At present we make an effort, do we not, in order to achieve a result, in order to arrive, to become something. If I am angry, ambitious, brutal, I make an effort not to be. But such effort is self-centered because I am still wanting to be something, perhaps negatively; there is still ambition, which is violence.

So if I am to change radically, without this self-centered motive, I must go very deeply into the problem of change. This means that I must think entirely differently, away from the collective, away from the ideal, away from the usual habit of discipline, practice, and all the rest of it. I must inquire who is the thinker, and what is thought, and find out whether thought is different from the thinker. Although thought has separated itself and set the thinker apart, he is still part of thought. And so long as thought is violent, mere control of thought by the thinker is of no value. So the question is: Can the mind be aware that it is violent, without dividing itself as the thinker who wants to get rid of violence?

This is really not a very complex problem. If you and I who are discussing it could go into it very carefully as individuals, we would see the extraordinary simplicity of it. Perhaps we are missing the significance of it because we think it is very complex. It is not. The simple fact is that there is no experiencer without the experience; the experiencer is the experience, the two are not separate. But so long as the experiencer sets himself apart and demands more experience, so long as he wishes to change this into that, there can be no fundamental transformation.

So the radical change we need is possible only when there are no ideals. Ideals are reform, and a mind that is merely reforming itself can never radically change. There can be no fundamental change if the mind is concerned with discipline, with fitting itself into a pattern, whether the pattern be that of society, of a teacher, or a pattern established by one's own thinking. There can be no radical change so long as the mind is thinking in terms of action according to its self-centered interest, however noble. The mere cultivation of virtue is not virtue.

So we have to inquire into the problem of change from a wholly different point of view. The totality of comprehension comes only when there is no division between the thinker and the thought—and that is an extraordinary experience. But you must come to it tentatively, with care, with inquiry, for mere acceptance or denial of the fact that the thought and the thinker are one will have no value. That is why a man who desires to bring about a fundamental change within himself must go into this problem very seriously and very deeply.

Question: Crime among young people is spreading everywhere. What can we do about it?

KRISHNAMURTI: You see, there is either a revolt within the pattern of society or a complete revolution outside of society. The complete revolution outside of society is what

I call religious revolution. Any revolution which is not religious is within society and is therefore no revolution at all, but only a modified continuation of the old pattern. What is happening throughout the world, I believe, is revolt within society, and this revolt often takes the form of what is called crime. There is bound to be this kind of revolt so long as our education is concerned only with training youth to fit into society—that is, to get a job, to earn money, to be acquisitive, to have more, to conform. That is what our so-called education everywhere is doing—teaching the young to conform, religiously, morally, economically; so naturally their revolt has no meaning, except that it must be suppressed, reformed, or controlled. Such revolt is still within the framework of society, and therefore it is not creative at all. But through right education, we could perhaps bring about a different understanding by helping to free the mind from all conditioning—that is, by encouraging the young to be aware of the many influences which condition the mind and make it conform.

So, is it possible to educate the mind to be aware of all the influences that now surround us, religious, economic, and social, and not be caught in any of them? I think it is, and when once we realize it, we shall approach this problem entirely differently.

Question: If we transform ourselves and become peaceful, while others do not transform themselves but remain aggressive and

brutal, are we not inviting them to attack and violate us as helpless victims?

KRISHNAMURTI: I wonder if this question is put seriously? Have you tried to transform yourself, to be really peaceful, and see what happens? Without actually being peaceful, we say to ourselves, "If I am peaceful, another may attack me," and so we set up the whole mechanism of attack and defense.

But surely, sirs, we are concerned, are we not, with the transformation of the individual, irrespective of what is done to him. We are not thinking in terms of nations, of groups, of races. So long as society exists as it is now, there must be attack and defense because the whole structure of our thinking is based on that. You are a German or a Muslim, and I am a Russian or a Hindu; being afraid of each other, we must be prepared to defend ourselves; therefore, we dare not be peaceful. So we keep that game going, and we live in its pattern. But now we are not talking as members of any particular society, of any particular group, nationality, or religion. We are talking as individual human beings. Any great thing, surely, is done by the individual, not by the mass, the collective.

The mass is composed of many individuals who are caught in words, slogans, in nationalism, in fear. But if you and I as individuals begin to think about the problem of peace, then we are not concerned with whether another is peaceful or not. Surely love is not a matter of your loving me, and therefore I love you. Love is something entirely different, is it not? Where there is love, there is no problem of the other. Similarly, when I know for myself what peace is, I am not concerned with whether others are going to attack me or not. They may. But my interest is in peace and the understanding of it, which means totally eliminating from myself the whole fabric of violence. And that requires tremendously clear thinking, deep meditation.

Question: You say the mind must be quiet, but it is always busy, night and day. How can I exchange it?

KRISHNAMURTI: I wonder if we are actually aware that our minds are busy night and day? Or is this merely a verbal statement? Are you fully conscious that your mind is ceaselessly active, or are you merely repeating a statement you have heard? And even if you know it directly for yourself, why do you wish to change it? Is it because someone has said you must have a quiet mind? If you want a quiet mind in order to achieve something more or to get somewhere else, then the acquisition of a quiet mind is just another form of self-centered action. So, does one see, without any motivation, that it is essential to have a quiet mind? If so, then the problem is: Can thought come to an end?

We know that when we are awake during the day, the mind is active with superficial things—with the job, the family, catching a train, and all the rest of it. And at night, in sleep, it is also active in dreams. So the process of thinking is going on ceaselessly. Now, can thought come to an end voluntarily, naturally, without being compelled through discipline? For only then can the mind be completely still. A mind that is made still, that is forced, disciplined to be still, is not a still mind; it is a dead mind.

So, can thought, which is incessantly active, come to an end? And if thought does come to an end, will this not be a complete death to the mind? Are we not therefore afraid of thought coming to an end? If thought should come to an end, what would happen?

The whole structure which we have built up of "myself" being important—my family, my country, my position, power, prestige—the whole of that would cease, obviously. So, do we really want to have a quiet mind?

If we do, then we must inquire, must we not, into the whole process of thinking; we must find out what thinking is. Is thinking merely the response of memory, or is thinking something else? If it is merely the response of memory, then can the mind put away all memory? Is it possible to put away all memory? That is, can thought cease to make an effort to retain the pleasant and discard the unpleasant memories?

Perhaps this all seems a bit too complex and difficult, but it is not, if you go into it. The state of a mind that is really silent is something extraordinary. It is not the silence of negation. On the contrary, a silent mind is a very intense mind. But for such a mind to come into being, we must inquire into the whole process of thinking. And thinking, for most of us, is the response of memory. All our education, all our upbringing, encourages the continuance of memory identified as the "me," and on that basis we set the ball of thought rolling.

So it is impossible to have a really still mind, a mind that is completely quiet, as long as you do not understand what thinking is and the whole structure of the thinker. Is there a thinker when there is not thought based on memory? To find out, you have to trace your thought, inquire into every thought that you have, not just verbally or casually, but very persistently, slowly, hesitantly, without condemning or justifying any thought. At present, there is a division between the thinker and the thought, and it is this division that creates conflict. Most of us are caught in conflict—perhaps not outwardly, but inwardly we are seething. We are in a continuous turmoil of wanting and not-wanting, of ambition, jealousy, anger, violence; and to have a really still, quiet mind, we must understand all that.

September 9, 1956

FOURTH TALK

Whatever may be our immediate problem, can we, through that problem, look at our life as a whole?

To understand what it is another is trying to convey, one must give a certain attention—not enforced attention or tremendous concentration, but that attention which comes with natural interest. After all, we have many problems in life—problems arising out of our relationship with society, the problems of war, of sex, of death, of whether or not there is God, and the problem of what this everlasting struggle is all about. We all have these problems. And I think we might begin to understand them deeply if we did not cling to one particular problem of our own, which is perhaps so close to us that it absorbs all our attention, all our effort, all our thinking, but tried instead to approach the problem of living as a whole. In understanding the problem of living as a whole, I think we shall be able to understand our personal problems.

That is what I want to deal with, if I can, this evening. Each one of us has a problem, and unfortunately that problem generally consumes most of our thought and energy. We are constantly groping, searching, trying to find an answer to our problem, and we want somebody else to supply that answer. It is probably for this very reason that you are here. But I do not think we will understand the totality of our existence if we merely look for an answer to a single problem. Because all problems are related; there is no isolated problem. So we have to look at life not as something to be broken up into parts, made fractional, but as something to be understood as a whole. If we can realize this, get the feeling of it, then I think we shall have a totally different approach to our individual problems, which are also the world problems.

What is happening now is that we are all so concerned with our own problems, with earning a livelihood, with getting ahead, with our personal virtue, and all the rest of it, that we do not have a general comprehension of the complete picture. And it seems to me that unless we get the feeling of the totality of our life with all its experiences, miseries, and struggles, unless we comprehend it as a whole, merely dealing with a particular problem, however apparently vital, will only create further problems, further misery.

I hope this is clear between us—that we are not considering one isolated problem, but we are trying to understand together the totality of the problem of our existence. So, whatever may be our immediate problem, can we, through that problem, look at our life as a whole? If we can, then I think the immediate problem which we have will undergo quite a change, and perhaps we shall be able to understand it and be free of it entirely.

Now, how does one set about to have this integrated outlook, this comprehensive view of life which reveals the significance of every relationship, every thought, every action? Surely, before we can see the whole picture, we must first be aware that we are always trying to solve our immediate problem in a very limited field. We want a particular answer, a satisfactory answer, an answer which will give us certainty. That is what we are seeking, is it not? And I think we must begin by being conscious of that; otherwise, we shall not be able to grasp the significance of this whole problem.

All this may at first seem very difficult; it may even sound rather absurd to those of you who are hearing it for the first time, and what we hear for the first time, we naturally tend to reject. But if one wants to understand, one must neither reject nor accept what is being said. One must examine it, not with sentimentality or intellectual preconceptions, but with that intelligence and common sense which will reveal the picture clearly.

So, why is it that most of us are incapable of looking at the whole picture of life, which, if understood, would resolve all our problems? We look at the picture of Germans or Russians or Hindus or what you will. We look at the picture with our knowledge, with our ideas, with a particular training or technique, with a mind which is conditioned. We are always translating the picture according to our background, according to our education, our tradition. We never look at the picture without this influence of the past, without thinking about the picture. Do you see what I mean? After all, if I want to understand something, I must come to it with a fresh mind, with a mind that is not burdened with accumulated experience, knowledge, with all the conditioning to which it has been subjected.

Life demands this, does it not? Life demands that I look at it afresh. Because life is movement, it is not a dead, static thing, and I must therefore approach it with a mind that is capable of looking at it without translating it in certain terms—as a Hindu, a Christian, or whatever it is I happen to be. So, before I can look at the whole picture, I must be aware of how my mind is burdened with knowledge, tradition, which prevents it from looking afresh at that which is moving, living. Knowledge, however wide, however necessary, at one level, does not bring comprehension of life, which is a constant movement. If my mind is burdened with technique, training, so that it can understand only that which is static, dead, then I can have no comprehension of life as a whole. To comprehend the totality of life, I must understand the process of knowledge, and how knowledge interferes with that comprehension. This is fairly obvious, is it not?—that knowledge interferes with the understanding of life.

And yet, what is happening in the world? All our education is a process of accumulating knowledge. We are concerned with developing techniques, with how to meditate, how to be good; the "how," the technique becomes knowledge, and with that we hope to understand the immeasurable. So when one says, "I understand what you are talking about," is it merely a verbal understanding, or has one really grasped the truth of the matter? If we really grasp the truth of what is being said, that very comprehension will free the mind from the accumulated knowledge which interferes with perception.

So, is it possible for one who has had many experiences, who has read the various philosophies, the learned books, who has accumulated information, knowledge, to put all that aside? I do not think one can put it aside, suppress, or deny it; but one can be aware of it, and not allow it to interfere with perception. After all, we are trying to find out what is truth, if there is reality, if there is God; and to discover this for oneself is true religion—not the acceptance of some silly ritual or dogma and all the rest of that nonsense.

To find something original and true, something timeless, you cannot come to it with the burden of memory, knowledge. The known, the past, can never help you to discover the moving, the creative. No amount of technique or learning, no amount of attending talks and discussions, can ever reveal to you the unknown. If you really see the truth of this, actually experience if for yourself, then you are free of all Masters and gurus, of all teachers, saints, and saviors. Because, they can only teach you what is known, and the mind which is burdened with the known can never find what is unknowable.

To be free from the known requires a great deal of understanding of the whole process of the accumulative mind. It would be silly to say, "I must forget the past"— that has no meaning. But if one begins to understand why the mind accumulates and treasures the past, why the whole momentum of the mind is based on time—if one begins to understand all that, then one will find that the mind can free itself from the past, from the burden of accumulated knowledge. There is then the discovery of something totally new, unexperienced, unimagined, which is a state of creativity and which may be called reality, God, or what you will.

So, being surrounded by problems, by innumerable conflicts, our difficulty is to know how to look at them, how to understand them, so that they are no longer a burden, and through those very problems we begin to discover the process by which the mind is everlastingly caught in time, in the known. Unless we can do that, our life remains very shallow. You may know a great deal, you may be a great scientist, you may be a great historian or just an ordinary person; but life will always be shallow, empty, dull, until you understand for yourself this whole process, which is really the beginning of self-knowledge.

So it seems to me that our many problems can never be solved until we approach them as an integral part of the totality of existence. We cannot understand the totality of existence as long as we break it up into compartments, as we are doing now. The difficulty is that our problems are so intense, so immediate, that we get caught in them; and not to be caught in them, the mind must begin to be aware of its own process of accumulation, by which it gains a sense of security for itself. After all, why do we accumulate property, money, position, knowledge, and so on? Obviously, because it gives us a sense of security. You may not have much property or money, but if you have knowledge, it gives you a feeling of security. It is only to the man who has no sense of security of any kind that the new is revealed because he is not concerned about himself and his achievements.

How is the mind to free itself from time? Time, after all, is knowledge. Time comes into being when there is the sense of achievement, something to be arrived at, something to be gained. "I am not important, but I shall be—in that idea, time has come into being, and with it the whole struggle of becoming. In the very idea, "I shall be," there is effort to become; and I think it is this effort to become which creates time, and which prevents a comprehension of the totality of things. You see, so long as I am thinking about myself in terms of gain and loss, I must have time. I must have time to cover the distance between now and tomorrow when I hope I shall be something, either in terms of virtue or position or knowledge. This creation of time breaks life up into segments, and that becomes the problem.

To understand the totality of this extraordinary thing called life, one must obviously not be too definite about these things. One cannot be definite with something which is so immense, which is not measurable by words. We cannot understand the immeasurable so long as we approach it through time.

To grasp the significance of all this is not an intellectual feat, nor a sentimental, emotional realization, but it means that you must really listen to what is being said; and in that very process of listening, you will find out for yourself that the mind, though it is the product of time, can go beyond time. But this demands very clear thinking, a great alertness of mind, in which no emotionalism is involved. To understand the immeasurable, the mind must be extraordinarily quiet, still; but if I think I am going to achieve stillness at some future date, I have destroyed the possibility of stillness. It is now or never. That is a very difficult thing to understand because we are all thinking of heaven in terms of time.

Question: Are yogic exercises helpful in any way to human beings?

KRISHNAMURTI: I think one must go into this question fairly deeply. Apparently in Europe as well as in India, there is this idea that by doing yogic exercises, practicing virtue, being good, participating in social work, reading sacred books, following a teacher—that by doing something of this kind, you are going to achieve salvation or enlightenment. I am afraid you are not. On the contrary, you are going to be caught in the things you are practicing, and therefore you will always be held a prisoner and your vision will be everlastingly limited.

Yogic exercises are all right, probably, for the body. Any kind of exercise—walking, jumping, climbing mountains, swimming, or whatever you do—is on the same level. But to suppose that certain exercises will lead you to salvation, to understanding, to God, truth, wisdom—this I think is sheer nonsense, even though all the yogis in India say otherwise. If once you see that any-thing that you practice, that you accept, that you develop, always has behind it the element of greed—wanting to get something, wanting to reach something, wanting to break a record—then you will leave it alone. A mind that is merely concerned with the "how," with doing yogic exercises, this or that, will only develop a sense of achievement through time, and such a mind can never comprehend that which is timeless.

After all, you practice yogic exercises in the hope of reaching something, gaining something; you hope to achieve happiness, bliss, or whatever is offered. Do you think bliss is so easily realized? Do you think it is something to be gained by doing certain exercises or developing concentration? Must not the mind be altogether free of this self-centered activity? Surely a man who practices yoga in order to reach enlightenment is concerned about himself, about his own growth; he is full of his own importance. So it is a tremendous art—an art which can be approached only through self-knowledge, not through any practice—to understand this whole process of self-centered activity in the name of God, in the name of truth, in the name of peace, or whatever it be—to understand and be free of it.

Now, to be free does not demand time, and I think this is our difficulty. We say, "I am envious, and to get rid of envy I must control, I must suppress, I must sacrifice, I must do penance, I must practice yoga," and all the rest of it—all of which indicates the continuance of self-centered activity, only transferred to a different level. If one sees this, if one really understands it, then one no longer thinks in terms of getting rid of envy in a certain period of time. Then the problem is: Can one get rid of envy immediately? It is like a hungry man—he does not want a promise of food tomorrow, he wants to be fed now, and in that sense he is free of time. But we are indolent, and what we want is a method to lead us to something that will ultimately give us pleasure.

Question: A well-known author has written a great deal about the use of certain drugs which enable man to arrive at some visionary experience of union with the divine ground. Are those experiences helpful in finding that state of which you speak?

KRISHNAMURTI: You can learn tricks or take drugs or get drunk, and you will have intense experiences of one kind or another, depressing or exciting. Obviously, the physiological condition does affect the psychological state of the mind, but drugs and practices of various kinds do not in any way bring about that state of which we are talking. All such things lead only to a variety, intensity, and diversity of experience—which we all want and hunger after because we are fed up with this world. We have had two world wars, with appalling misery and everlasting strife on every side, and our own minds are so petty, personal, limited. We want to escape from all this, either through psychology, philosophy, so-called religion, or through some exercise or drug—they are all on the same level.

The mind is seeking a sensation; you want to experience what you call reality or God, something immense, great, vital. You want to have visions, and if you take some kind of drug or are sufficiently conditioned in a certain religion, you will have visions. The man who is everlastingly thinking about Christ or Buddha or what not will sooner or later have experiences, visions. But that is not truth; it has nothing whatever to do with reality. Those are all self-projections; they are the result of your demand for experience. Your own conditioning is projecting what you want to see.

To find out what is real, the mind must cease to demand any experience. So long as you are craving experience, you will have it, but it will not be real— real in the sense of the timeless, the immeasurable; it will not have the perfume of reality. It will all be an illusion, the product of a mind that is frustrated, that is seeking a thrill, an emotion, a feeling of vitality. That is why you follow leaders. They are always promising something new, a utopia, always sacrificing the present for the future, and you foolishly follow them because it is exciting. You have had that experience in this country, and you ought to know better than anyone else the miseries, the brutality of it all. Most of us demand the same kind of experience, the same kind of sensation, only at another level. That is why we take various drugs, or perform ceremonies, or practice some exercise that acts as a stimulant. These things all have significance in the sense that their use indicates that one is still craving experience; therefore, the mind is everlastingly agitated. And the mind that is agitated, that is craving experience, can never find out what is true.

Truth is always new, totally unknown, and unknowable. The mind must come to it without any demand, without any knowledge, without any wish; it must be empty, completely naked. Then only truth may happen. But you cannot invite it.

Question: Is our life predetermined, or is the way of life to be freely chosen?

KRISHNAMURTI: So long as we have choice, surely there is no freedom. Please follow this; do not merely reject or accept it, but let us think it out together. The mind that is capable of choosing is not free because in choice there is always conflict, conscious or unconscious, and a mind that is in conflict is never free. Our life is full of conflict; we are always choosing between good and bad, between this and that; you know this very well. We are always comparing, judging, evaluating, accepting, rejecting—that is the process of our life, which is a constant struggle, and a mind that is struggling is never free.

And are we individuals—individuals in the sense of being unique? Are we? Or are we merely the result of our conditioning, of innumerable influences, of centuries of tradition? You may like to separate yourself as being of the West, and set yourself still further apart as being German. But are you an individual in the sense of being completely uncorrupted, uninfluenced? Only in that state are you free—not otherwise. Which does not mean anarchy or selfishly individual existence—on the contrary.

But now you are not individuals; you are anything but that. You are German, English, French; you are Catholics, Protestants, communists—something or other. You are stamped, shaped, held within the framework in which you have been brought up, or which you have subsequently chosen. So your life is predetermined. You saw ten years ago how your life was predetermined. And every Catholic, every churchgoer, every person who belongs to any religious organization—his life is predetermined, fixed; therefore, he is never free. He may talk about freedom, he may talk about love and peace, but he cannot have love and peace, nor can he be free because for him those are mere words.

Your life is shaped, controlled by the society which you have created. You have created the wars, the leaders; you have created the organized religions of which you are now slaves. So your life is predetermined. And to be free, you must first be aware that your life is predetermined, that it is conditioned, that all your responses are more or less the same as those of everybody else throughout the world. Superficially, your responses may be different; you may respond one way here, another way in India or in China, and so on, but fundamentally you are held in the framework of your particular conditioning, and you are never an individual. Therefore it is absurd to talk about freedom and self-determination. You can choose between blue cloth and red cloth, and that is about all; your freedom is on that level. If you go into it very deeply, you will find that you are not an individual at all.

But by going into it very deeply, you will also find that you can be free from all this conditioning—as a German, as a Catholic, as a Hindu, as a believer or a nonbeliever. You can be free from it all. Then you will know what it is to have an innocent mind, and it is only such a mind that can find out what is truth.

Question: Will awareness free us, as you suggest, from our undesirable qualities?

KRISHNAMURTI: I think it is important to understand what we mean by awareness. I am going to explain what I mean, and please do not add something mysterious, complicated, or mystical. It is very clear and simple if one cares to go right to the end of it.

We are aware, are we not, of many things. You are aware that I am standing here, that I am talking, and that you are listening. And if you are alert, you are also aware of how you are listening. To know how you are listening is also part of awareness, and it is very important, because if you are aware of how you are listening, you will know in what way you are conditioned. You are probably interpreting what is being said according to your conditioning, according to your prejudices, according to your knowledge; and when you are interpreting, you are not listening. To be conscious of all this is part of awareness, is it not?

Now if you go still further, you will find that the moment you are really listening and not interpreting according to your prejudices, you begin to see for yourself what is true and what is false. Because true and false are not a matter of prejudice or opinion; either it is so or it is not. But if you are concerned with interpretation all the time, then your vision is blurred and there is no clear perception. That is why most of us are not really listening to what is being said—because we are interpreting it in terms of our upbringing or preconceptions. If you are a Christian, you listen and compare what is being said with the teaching of the Bible or the Christ; or if you do not do that, you refer to some other information which you have gathered. So you are always listening with a barrier. To see this whole process going on in one's mind is part of awareness, is it not?

The questioner wants to know if through awareness he can be free of any unpleasant qualities. That is, can one be free, let us say, of envy? If you will follow what I am saying, you will see the full implication of what lies in this question.

Most of us, if we are at all aware, cognizant, conscious of ourselves, know when we are envious. Furthermore, we can see that our whole society is based on envy, and that religions are also based on it—wanting something more, not only in this world, but also in the next. We know the feeling of being envious, the superficial as well as the very complex process of envy.

Now, being aware of envy, what happens? We either condemn or rationalize it. We generally condemn it because to condemn is part of our upbringing; we are educated to condemn envy; it is the thing to do, even though we are envious all the time. By condemning envy, we hope to be free of it, but we are not free; it keeps on returning. Envy exists so long as there is a comparative mind. When I am comparing myself with somebody who is greater, more popular, more virtuous and so on, I am envious. So a comparative mind breeds envy.

And you will see, if you go into this problem still deeper, that so long as you verbalize that feeling by calling it envy, the feeling goes on. I hope you are following this. You name the feeling, do you not? You say, "I am envious." But cannot one know that one is envious without naming it? Is it only by naming the feeling that one becomes conscious of it?

How do you know you are envious? Please take it very simply, and you will see. Do you know it only after you have given a name to it, calling it envy? Or do you know it as a feeling, independent of all terms? Is not all this also part of awareness?

Let us go slowly. I am envious, and I condemn it because to condemn envy is part of my social upbringing, but it goes on. So if I really want to be free of envy, what am I to do? That is the problem. I do not want the feeling to continue because that would be too silly; I see the absurdity of it, and I want to be free of it. So, how is the mind to be free of envy? First, I have to see that all comparison must cease, and to really see that requires very arduous inquiry, because one's whole upbringing is based on comparison— you must be as good as your brother or your uncle or your grandfather or Jesus or whoever it is. So, can the mind cease to compare?

Then the problem is: When one has a certain feeling, can the mind stop naming it, stop calling it envy? If you will experiment with this, you will see how extraordinarily alert the mind must be to differentiate the word from the feeling. All this is part of awareness, in which no effort is involved, because the moment you make an effort, you have a motive or gain, and therefore you are still envious.

So the mind is envious as long as it is comparing itself with somebody else, and it is envious as long as it gives a name to the feeling, calling it envy, because by giving it a name, it strengthens that feeling. And when the mind does not compare, when the mind does not give a name to the feeling and thereby strengthen it, you will find, if you proceed very hesitantly, carefully, diligently, that awareness does free the mind from envy.

September 14, 1956

FIFTH TALK

What happens if we do not escape?
Can the mind go into that?

I think these meetings will be useless if what we are discussing is regarded merely as a verbal communication without much significance. Most of us, it seems to me, listen rather casually to something very serious, and we have little time or inclination to give our thought to the profound things of life and go deeply into them for ourselves. We are inclined to accept or to deny very easily. But if, during these meetings, instead of just listening superficially, we can actually experience what we are talking about as we go along, then I think it will be worthwhile to discuss a problem which must be confronting most of us. I am referring to the problem of dependence. It is really a very complex problem, but if we can go into it deeply and not merely listen to the verbal description, if each one of us can be aware of it, see the whole implication of dependence and where it leads, then perhaps we shall discover for ourselves whether man, you and I, can be totally free from dependence.

I think dependence, in its deeper psychological aspects, corrupts our thinking and our lives; it breeds exploitation; it cultivates authority, obedience, a sense of acceptance without understanding. And if we are to bring about a totally new kind of religion, entirely different from what religion is now, if there is to be the total revolution of a truly religious person, then I think we must understand the tremendous significance of dependence and be free of it.

Most of us are dependent, not only on society, but on our neighbor, on our immediate relationship with wife, husband, children, or on some authority. We rely on another for our conduct, for our behavior, and in the process of dependence, we identify ourselves with a class, with a race, with a country; this psychological dependence does bring about a sense of frustration. Surely it must have occurred to some of us to ask ourselves whether one can ever be psychologically, inwardly free—free in one's heart and mind of all dependence on another.

Obviously, we are all interdependent in our everyday physical existence; our whole structure is based on physical interdependence, and it is natural, is it not, to depend on others in that sense. But I think it is totally unnatural to depend on another for our psychological comfort, for our inward security and well being.

If we are at all aware of this process of dependence, we can see what it involves. There is in it a great sense of fear, which ultimately leads to frustration. Psychological dependence on another gives a false sense of security. And if it is not a person on whom we depend, it is a belief or an ideal or a country or an ideology or the accumulation of knowledge.

We see, then, that psychologically we do depend. I think this is fairly obvious to any person who is at all aware of himself in his relationship with another and with society.

Now, why do we depend? And is it possible not to depend psychologically, to be free of this inward dependence of one mind on another? I think it is fairly important to find out why we depend. And if we did not depend, what would happen? Is it a feeling of loneliness, a sense of emptiness, insufficiency that drives us to depend on something? Are we dependent because we lack self-confidence? And if we do have confidence in ourselves, does that bring about freedom, or merely an aggressive, self-assertive activity?

I do not know if you think, as I do, that this is a significant problem in life. Perhaps we are not aware of our psychological dependence; but if we are, we are bound to see that behind this dependence, there is immense fear, and it is to escape from that fear that we depend. Psychologically, we do not want to be disturbed or to have taken away from us that on which we depend, whether it be a country, an idea, or a person; therefore, that on which we depend becomes very important in our life and we are always defending it.

It is in order to escape from the fear which we unconsciously know exists in us that we turn to another to give us comfort, to give us love, to encourage us—and that is the very process of dependence. So, can the mind be free of this dependence and thus be able to look at the whole problem of fear? Without deeply understanding fear and being free of it, the mere search for reality, for God, for happiness is utterly useless because what you are seeking then becomes that on which you again depend. Only the mind that is inwardly free of fear can know the blessing of reality, and the mind can be free of fear only when there is no dependence.

Now, can we look at fear? What is fear? Fear exists, surely, only in relation to something. Fear does not exist by itself. And what is it that we are afraid of? We may not be consciously aware of our fear, but unconsciously we are afraid, and that unconscious fear has far greater power over our daily thoughts and activities than the effort we make to suppress or deny fear.

So, what is it that most of us are afraid of? There are superficial fears, such as the fear of losing a job, and so on, but to those fears we can generally adjust ourselves. If you lose your job, you will find some other way of making a living. The great fear is not for one's social security; it lies much deeper than that. And I do not know if the mind is willing to look at itself so profoundly as to be able to find out for itself what it is intrinsically frightened of. Unless you discover for yourself the deep source of your fear, all efforts to escape from fear, all cultivation of virtue, and so on is of no avail because fear is at the root of most of our anxious urges. So can we find out what it is we are afraid of, each one of us? Is the cause of fear common to us all, like death? Or is it something that each one of us has to discover, look at, go into for himself?

Most of us are frightened of being lonely. We are unconsciously aware that we are empty, that we are nothing. Though we may have titles, jobs, position, power, money, and all the rest of it, underlying all that there is a state of emptiness, an unfulfilled longing, a vacuum which we translate as loneliness—that state in which the self, the "me," has completely enclosed the mind. Perhaps that is the very root of our fear. And can we look at it in order to understand it? For I think we must understand it if we would go beyond it.

Most of our activity is based on fear, is it not? That is, we never want to face ourselves exactly as we are, to know ourselves completely. And the more deeply and drastically you go into yourself, the greater the sense of emptiness you will find. All that we have learned—the knowledge we have acquired, the virtues we have cultivated—all this is on the surface, and it has very little meaning if one penetrates more and more deeply into oneself, for as one penetrates, one comes upon this enormous sense of emptiness. You may sometimes have caught a fleeting glimpse of it as a feeling of loneliness, of insufficiency, but then you turn on the radio, or talk, or do something else to escape from that feeling. And that feeling, that sense of "not-being," may be the cause of fear.

I think most of us have, at rare moments, experienced that state. And when we do fleetingly experience it, we generally run away from it through some form of amusement, through knowledge, through the vast mechanism of escape offered by the so-called civilized world. But what happens if we do not escape? Can the mind go into that? I think it must. Because in going deeply into that state of emptiness, we may discover something totally new and be completely free of fear.

To understand something, we must approach it without any sense of condemnation, must we not? If I want to understand you, I must not be full of memories; my mind must not be burdened with knowledge about

Germans, Hindus, Russians, or whatever the label may be. To understand, I must be free of all sense of condemnation and evaluation. Similarly, if I am to understand this state which I have called emptiness, loneliness, a feeling of insufficiency, I must look at it without any sense of condemnation. If I want to understand a child, I must not condemn him or compare him with another child. I must observe him in all his moods—when he is playing, crying, eating, talking. In such a manner the mind must watch the feeling of emptiness, without any sense of condemnation or rejection. Because, the moment I condemn or reject that feeling, I have already created the barrier of fear.

So, can one look at oneself, and at this sense of insufficiency, without any condemnation? After all, condemnation is a process of verbalization, is it not? And when one condemns, there is no true communication.

I hope you are following this because I think it is very important to understand it now, to really experiment with it as you are listening, and not merely go away and think about it later. This does not mean experimenting with what I say, but experimenting with the discovery of your own loneliness, your own emptiness—the feeling of insufficiency which causes fear. And you cannot be free to discover if you approach that state with any sense of condemnation.

So, can we now look at that thing which we have called emptiness, loneliness, insufficiency, realizing that we have always tried to escape from it rather than comprehend it? I see that what is important is to understand it, and that I cannot understand it if there is any sense of condemnation. So condemnation goes; therefore, I approach it with a totally different mind, a whole, free mind. Then I see that the mind cannot separate itself from emptiness because the mind itself is that emptiness. If you really go into it very deeply for yourself, free of all condemnation, you will find that out of the thing which we have called emptiness, insufficiency, fear, there comes an extraordinary state, a state in which the mind is completely quiet, undemanding, unafraid; and in that silence there is the coming into being of creativity, reality, God, or whatever you may like to call it. This inward sense of having no fear can take place only when you understand the whole process of your own thinking, and then I think it is possible to discover for oneself that which is eternal.

Question: Most of us are caught up in and are bored with the routine of our work, but our livelihood depends on it. Why can we not be happy in our work?

KRISHNAMURTI: Surely, modern civilization is making many of us do work which we as individuals do not like at all. Society as it is now constituted, being based on competition, ruthlessness, war, demands, let us say, engineers and scientists; they are wanted everywhere throughout the world because they can further develop the instruments of war and make the nation more efficient in its ruthlessness. So education is largely dedicated to building the individual into an engineer or a scientist, whether he is fit for it or not. The man who is being educated as an engineer may not really want to be one. He may want to be a painter, a musician, or who knows what else. But circumstances—education, family tradition, the demands of society, and so on—force him to specialize as an engineer. So we have created a routine in which most of us get caught, and then we are frustrated, miserable, unhappy for the rest of our lives. We all know this.

It is fundamentally a matter of education, is it not? And can we bring about a different kind of education in which each person, the teacher as well as the student, loves what he is doing? *Loves*—I mean exactly that word. But you cannot love what you are doing if you are all the time using it as a means to success, power, position, prestige.

Surely, as it is now constituted, society does produce individuals who are utterly bored, who are caught in the routine of what they are doing. So it will take a tremendous revolution, will it not, in education and in everything else, to bring about a totally different environment—an environment which will help the students, the children, to grow in that which they really love to do.

As things are now, we have to put up with routine, with boredom, and so we try to escape in various ways. We try to escape through amusements, through television or the radio, through books, through so-called religion, and so our lives become very shallow, empty, dull. This shallowness, in turn, breeds the acceptance of authority, which gives us a sense of universality, of power, position. We know all this in our hearts, but it is very difficult to break away from it all because to break away demands, not the usual sentimentality, but thought, energy, hard work.

So if you want to create a new world—and surely you must after these terrible wars, after the misery, the terrors that human beings have gone through—then there will have to be a religious revolution in each one of us, a revolution that will bring about a new culture and a totally new religion, which is not the religion of authority, of priest-craft, of dogma and ritual. To create a wholly different kind of society, there must be this religious revolution—that is, a revolution within the individual, and not the terrible outward bloodshed, which only brings more tyranny, more misery and fear. If we are to create a new world—new in a totally different sense—then it must be our world, and not a German world or a Russian world or a Hindu world, for we are all human beings, and the earth is ours.

But unfortunately very few of us feel deeply about all this because it demands love, not sentimentality or emotionalism. Love is hard to find, and the man who is sentimentally emotional is generally cruel. To bring about a totally different culture, it seems to me that there must take place in each one of us this religious revolution, which means that there must be freedom, not only from all creeds and dogmas, but freedom from personal ambition and self-centered activity. Only then, surely, can there be a new world.

Question: You reject discipline and outward order and suggest that we should act only by inner impulse. Will this not add to

the great instability of people and encourage the following of irresponsible urges, especially among the youth of our time, who only want to enjoy themselves and are already drifting?

KRISHNAMURTI: I am afraid the questioner has not understood what we are talking about at all. I am not suggesting that you should abandon discipline. Even if you did try to abandon it, your society, your neighbor, your wife or husband, the people around you would force you to discipline yourself again. We are discussing not the abandonment of discipline but the whole problem of discipline. If we could understand the very deep implications of discipline, then there might be order, which is not based on coercion, compulsion, fear.

Surely, discipline implies suppression, does it not? Please think it out with me and do not just reject it. I know you are all very fond of discipline, of obeying, following, but do not merely reject what I am suggesting. In disciplining myself, I suppress what I want in order to conform to some greater value, to the edicts of society, or whatever it is. That suppression may be a necessity, or it may be voluntary, even pleasurable, but it is still a form of putting away desire of one kind or another—suppressing it, denying it, and training myself to conform to a pattern laid down by society, by a teacher, or by the sanctions of a particular regime. If we reject that outward form of discipline, then we establish a discipline of our own. We say, "I must not do this, it is wrong; I must do only what is right, what is good, what is noble. When I have an ugly thought, I must suppress it; I must discipline myself, I must practice constant watchfulness."

Now, where there is conformity, discipline, suppression, conscious or unconscious, there is a constant struggle going on, is there not? We are all familiar with this fact. I am not saying anything new, but we are directly examining what is constantly taking place. And a mind that is suppressed, compelled to conform, must ultimately break out into all kinds of chaotic activities—which is what actually happens.

When we discipline ourselves, it is in order to get something we want. After all, the so-called religious people discipline themselves because they are pursuing an idea in the distance which they hope someday to achieve. The idealist, the utopian, is thinking in terms of tomorrow; he has established the ideal for the future and is always trying to conform to what he thinks he should be. He never understands the whole process of what is actually taking place in himself, but is only concerned with the ideal. The "what should be" is the pattern, and he is trying to fit himself into it because he hopes in that pattern there will be greater happiness, greater bliss, the discovery of truth, God, and all the rest of it.

So, is it not important to find out why the mind disciplines itself, and not merely say that it should not? I think there would be not conformity, not enforcement, but a totally different kind of adjustment if we could really understand what it is the mind is seeking through discipline. After all, you discipline yourself in order to be safe. Is that not essentially true? You want to be secure, not only in this world, but also in the next world—if there is a next world. The mind that is seeking security must conform, and conformity means discipline. You want to find a Master, a teacher, and so you discipline yourself, you meditate, you suppress certain desires, you force your mind to fit into a frame. And so your whole life, your whole consciousness is twisted.

If we understand, not superficially, but really deeply, the inward significance of discipline, we will see that it makes the mind conform, as a soldier is made to conform; and the mind that merely conforms to a pattern, however noble, can obviously never be free, and therefore can never perceive what is true. This does not mean that the mind can do whatever it likes. When it does whatever it likes, it soon finds out there is always pain, sorrow, at the end of it. But if the mind sees the full significance of all this, then you will find that there is immediate understanding without compulsion, without suppression.

One of our difficulties is that we have been so trained, educated to suppress, to conform, that we are really frightened of being free; we are afraid that in freedom we may do something ugly. But if we begin to understand the whole pattern of discipline, which is to see that we conform in order to arrive, to gain, to be secure, then we shall find that there comes into being a totally different process of awareness in which there is no necessity for suppression or conformity.

Question: What happens after death? And do you believe in reincarnation?

KRISHNAMURTI: This is a very complex problem that touches every human being whether he is young or old, and whether he lives in Russia, where there is officially no belief in the hereafter, or in India, or here in the West, where there is every shade of belief. It really requires very careful inquiry and not merely the acceptance or rejection of a particular belief. So let us please think it out together very carefully.

Death is the inevitable end for all of us, and we know it. We may rationalize it or escape from the uncertainty of that vast unknown through belief in reincarnation, resurrection, or what you will, but fear is still there. The body, the physical organism, inevitably wears itself out, just as every machine wears itself out. You and I know that disease, accident, or old age will come and carry us away. We say, "Yes, that is so," and we accept it, so that is really not our problem. Our problem is much deeper. We are frightened of losing everything that we have gained, understood, gathered; we are frightened of not-being; we are frightened of the unknown. We have lived; we have accumulated, learned, experienced, suffered; we have educated the mind and disciplined ourselves, and is death the end of it all? We do not like to think that it is. So we say there must be a hereafter; life must continue, if not by returning to earth, then it must continue elsewhere. And many of us have a comforting belief in the theory of reincarnation.

To me, belief is not important because belief in an idea, in a theory, however comforting, however satisfactory, does not give understanding of the full significance of death. Surely, death is something totally unknown, completely new. However anxiously I may inquire into death, it ever remains something which I do not know. All that you and I know is the past, and the continuity of the past through the present to the future. Memory identified with my house, my family, my name, my acquisitions, virtues, struggles, experiences—all that is the "me," and we want the "me" to continue. Or, if you are tired of the "me," you say, "Thank God, death ends it all," but that does not solve the problem either.

So we must find out, surely, the truth of this matter. What you happen to believe or disbelieve about reincarnation has no truth in it. But instead of asking what happens after death, can we not discover the truth of what death is? Because life itself may be a process of death. Why do we divide life from death? We do so because we think life is a process of continuity, of accumulation, and death is cessation, the annihilation of all that we have accumulated. So we have separated living from death. But life may be entirely different; it may be a process the truth of which we do not know, a process of living and dying each minute. All that we know is a form of continuity—what I was yesterday, what I am today, and what I hope to be tomorrow. That is all we know. And because the mind clings to that continuity, it is afraid of what it calls death.

Now, can the living mind know death? Do you understand the problem? It is not a question of what happens after death, but can a living mind—a mind that is not diseased, that is fully alert, aware—experience that state which it calls death? Which means, really, do we know what living is? Because living may be dying, in the sense of dying to our memories. Please follow this, and perhaps you will see the enormous implication of this idea of death.

We live in the field of the known, do we not? The known is that with which I have identified myself—my family, my country, my experiences, my job, my friends, the virtues, the qualities, the knowledge I have gathered, all the things I have known. So the mind is the result of the past; the mind is the past. The mind is burdened with the known. And can the mind free itself from the known? That is, can I die to all that I have accumulated—not when I am a doddering old man, but now? While I am still full of vitality, clarity, and understanding, can I die to everything that I have been, that I am going to be, or think that I should be? That is, can I die to the known, die to every moment? Can I invite death, enter the house of death while living?

You can enter the house of death only when the mind is free from the known—the known being all that you have gathered, all that you are, all that you think you are and hope to be. All this must completely cease. And is there then a division between living and dying, or only a totally different state of mind?

If you are merely listening to the words, then I am afraid you will not understand the implication of what is being said. But if you will, you can see for yourself that living is a process of dying every minute, and renewing. Otherwise you are not really living, are you? You are merely continuing a state of mind within the field of the known, which is routine, which is boredom. There is living, surely, only when you die—consciously, intelligently, with full awareness—to everything that you have been, to the many yesterdays. Then the problem of death is entirely different. There may be no problem at all. There may be a state of mind in which time does not exist. Time exists only when there is identification with the known. The mind that is burdened with the known is everlastingly afraid of the unknown. Whatever it may do, whatever may be its beliefs, its dogmas, its hopes, they are all based on fear, and it is this fear that corrupts living.

September 15, 1956

SIXTH TALK

Can the mind, without any form of compulsion, without a motive, bring about a transformation within itself?

It seems to me that the whole world is intent on capturing the mind of man. We have created the psychological world of relationship, the world in which we live, and it, in turn, is controlling us, shaping our thinking, our activities, our psychological being. Every political and religious organization, you will find, is after the mind of man—"after" in the sense of wanting to capture it, shape it to a certain pattern. The powers that be in the communist world are blatantly conditioning the mind of man in every direction, and this is also true of the organized religions throughout the world, which for centuries have tried to mold the way of man's thought. Each specialized group, whether religious, secular, or political is striving to draw and to hold man within the pattern of that which its books, its leaders, the few in power, think is good for him. They think they know the future; they think they know what is the ultimate good for man. The priests, with their so-called religious authority, as well as the worldly powers—whether it be in Rome, in Moscow, in America, or elsewhere—are all trying to control man's thought process, are they not? And most of us eagerly accept some form of authority and subject ourselves to it. There are very few who escape the clutches of this organized control of man and his thinking.

Merely to break away from a particular religious pattern, or from a political pattern of the left or of the right, in order to adopt another pattern, or to establish one of our own, will not, it seems to me, simplify the extraordinary complexity of our lives, or resolve the catastrophic misery in which most of us live. I think the fundamental solution lies elsewhere, and it is this fundamental solution that we are all trying to find. Groping blindly, we join this organization or that. We belong to a particular society, follow this or that leader, try to find a Master in India or somewhere else—always hoping to break away from our narrow, limited existence, but always caught, it seems to me, in this conflict within the pattern. We never seem to get away from the pattern, either self-created or imposed by some leader or religious authority. We blindly accept authority in the hope of breaking through the cloud of our own strife, misery, and struggle, but no leader, no authority is ever going to free man. I think history has shown this very clearly, and you in this country know it very well—perhaps better than others.

So if a new world is to come into being, as it must, it seems to me extremely important to understand this whole process of authority—the authority imposed by society, by the book, by a set of people who think they know the ultimate good for man and who seek to force him through torture, through every form of compulsion, to conform to their pattern. We are quick to follow such people because in our own being we are so uncertain, so confused, and we also follow because of our vanity and arrogance and out of desire for the power offered by another.

Now, is it possible to break away from this whole pattern of authority? Can we break away from all authority of any kind in ourselves? We may reject the authority of another, but unfortunately we still have the authority of our own experience, of our own knowledge, of our own thinking, and that, in turn, becomes the pattern which guides us, yet that is essentially no different from the authority of another. There is this desire to follow, to imitate, to conform in the hope of achieving something greater, and so long as this desire exists, there must be misery and strife, every form of suppression, frustration, and suffering.

I do not think we sufficiently realize the necessity of being free of this compulsion to follow authority, inward or outward. And I think it is very important psychologically to understand this compulsion; otherwise, we shall go on blindly struggling in this world in which we live and have our being, and we shall never find that other thing which is so infinitely greater. We must surely break away from this world of imitation and conformity if we are to find a totally different world. This means a really fundamental change in our lives—in the way of our action, in the way of our thought, in the way of our feeling.

But most of us are not concerned with that; we are not concerned with understanding our thoughts, our feelings, our activities. We are only concerned with what to believe or not to believe, with whom to follow or not to follow, with which is the right society or political party, and all the rest of that nonsense. We are never concerned deeply, inwardly, with a radical change in the way of our daily life, in the way of our speech, the sensitivity of our thought towards another—we are not concerned with any of that. We cultivate the intellect and acquire knowledge of innumerable things, but we remain inwardly the same— ambitious, cruel, violent, envious, burdened with all the pettiness of which the mind is capable. And seeing all this, is it possible to break away from the petty mind? I think that is the only real problem. And I think that in breaking away from the petty mind, we shall find the right answer to our economic, social, and other problems.

Without understanding the pettiness of ourselves, the narrow, shallow thoughts and feelings that we have— without going into that very deeply and fundamentally, merely to join societies and follow leaders who promise better health, better economic conditions, and all the rest of it, seems to me so utterly immature. Our fear may perhaps be modified, moved to another level, but inwardly we remain the same; there is still fear and the sense of frustration that goes with self-centered activity. Unless we fundamentally change that, do what we will—create the most extraordinary legislative order, bring about a welfare state which guarantees everyone's social well being and all the rest of it—inwardly we shall always remain poor.

So how is the mind to break away from its own pettiness? I do not know if you have ever thought about this, or if it is a problem to you. Perhaps you are merely concerned with improving conditions, bringing about certain reforms, establishing a better social order, and are not concerned with a radical change in human thinking. It seems to me that the real problem is whether a fundamental change comes about through outward circumstances, or through any form of compulsion, or whether it comes from a totally different direction. If we rely on any form of compulsion, on outward changes in the social order, on so-called education, which is the mere gathering of information, and so on, surely our lives will still be shallow. We may know a great deal about many things, we may be able to quote the various authorities and be very learned in the expression of our thought, but our minds will be as petty as before, with the same ache of deep anxiety, uncertainty, fear. So there is no fundamental transformation through outward change, or through any form of pressure, influence. Fundamental transformation comes from quite a different direction, and this is what I would like briefly to talk about, even though I have already talked about it a great deal during the last five meetings, because it seems to me that this is the only real issue.

So long as we ourselves are confused, small, petty, whatever our activity may be, and whatever concept we may have of truth, of God, of beauty or love, our thinking and our action are bound to be equally petty, confused, limited. A confused mind can only think in terms of confusion. A petty mind can never imagine what God is, what truth is, and yet that is what we are occupied with. So it seems to me important to discover whether the mind can transform itself without any compulsion, without any motive. The moment there is compulsion, the mind is already conforming to a pattern. If there is a motive for change, that motive is self-projected; therefore, the change, being a product of self-centered activity, is no change at all. It seems to me that this is the real thing which we have fundamentally to tackle, put our teeth into—and not whom to follow, who is the best leader, and all that rubbish.

The question is: Can the mind, without any form of compulsion, without a motive, bring about a transformation within itself? A motive is bound to be the result of self-centered desire, and such a motive is self-enclosing; therefore, there is no freedom, there is no transformation of the mind. So, can the mind break away from all influence and from all motive? And is not this very breaking away from all influence and from all motive in itself a transformation of the mind? Do you follow what I mean?

You see, we must abandon this world in which we are caught—the world of authority, of power, of influence, the world of conditioning, of fear, of ambition and envy—if we are to find the other world. We must let this world go, let it die in us without compulsion, without motive, because any motive will be a mere repetition of the same thing in different terms.

I think just to look at the problem, just to comprehend the problem, brings its own answer. I see that, as a human being, I am the result of innumerable influences, social compulsions, religious impressions, and that if I try to find reality, truth, or God, that very search will be based on the things I have been taught, shaped by what I have known, conditioned by my education and by the influences of the environment in which I live. So, can I be free of all that? To be free, I must first know for myself that my mind is conditioned, that is, I must be fully aware that I am not really a human being, but a Hindu, a Catholic, a German, a Protestant, a communist, a socialist, or whatever it may be. I am born with a label, and this, or some other label of my own choosing, sticks to me for the rest of my life. I am born and die in one religion, or I change from one religion to another, and I think I have understood reality, God, but I have only perpetuated the conditioned mind, the label. Now, can I, as a human being, put all that away from me without any compulsion?

I think it is very important to understand that any effort made to free oneself from one's conditioning is another form of conditioning. If I try to free myself from Hinduism, or any other -ism, I am making that effort in order to achieve what I consider to be a more desirable state; therefore, the motive to change, conditions the change. So I must realize my own conditioning and do absolutely nothing. This is very difficult. But I must know for myself that my mind is small, petty, confused, conditioned, and see that any effort to change it is still within the field of that confusion; therefore, any such effort only breeds further confusion.

I hope I am making this clear. If your mind is confused, as the minds of most people are, then your thought, your action, and your choice of a leader will also be confused. But if you know that you are confused, and realize that any effort born of that confusion can only bring still further confusion, then what happens? If you are fundamentally, deeply aware of that fact, then you will see quite a different process at work. It is not the process of effort; there is no wanting to break through your confusion. You know that you are totally confused, and therefore there is the cessation of all thinking.

This is a very difficult thing to comprehend because we are so certain that thinking, rationalizing, logical reasoning, can resolve our problems. But we have never really examined the process of thinking. We assume that thinking will solve our problems, but we have never gone into the whole issue of what thinking is. So long as I remain a Hindu, a Christian, or what you will, my thinking must be shaped by that pattern; therefore, my thinking, my whole response to life, is conditioned. So long as I think as an Indian, a German, or whatever it is and act according to that petty, nationalistic background, it inevitably leads to separation, to hatred, to war and misery. So we have to inquire into the whole problem of thinking.

There is no freedom of thought because all thought is conditioned. There is freedom only when I understand that all thought is conditioned and am therefore free of that conditioning—which means, really, that there is no thought at all, no thinking in terms of Catholic, Hindu, Buddhist, German, or what you will, but pure observation, complete attention. In this, I think, lies the real revolution—in the immense understanding that thought does not solve the problem of existence. Which does not mean that you must become thoughtless. On the contrary, to understand the process of thinking requires not acceptance or denial but intense inquiry. When the mind understands the whole process of itself, there is then a fundamental revolution, a radical change which is not brought about through conscious effort. It is an effortless state, out of which comes a total transformation.

But this transformation is not of time. It is not a thing about which you can say to yourself, "It will come eventually; I must work at it, I must do this and not that." On the contrary, the moment you introduce time as a factor of change, there is no real change at all.

The immeasurable is not of this world; it is not put together by the mind because what the mind has put together, the mind can undo. To understand the immeasurable, which is to enter into a different world altogether, we must understand this world in which we live, this world which we have created and of which we are a part—the world of ambition, greed, envy, hatred, the world of separation, fear, and lust. That means we must understand ourselves, the unconscious as well as the conscious, and this is not very difficult if you set your mind to it. If you really want to know the totality of your own being, you can easily discover it. It reveals itself in every relationship, at every moment—when you are entering the bus, getting a taxi, or talking to someone.

But most of us are not concerned with that because it requires serious endeavor, persistent inquiry. Most of us are very superficial; we are easily satisfied with such words as God, love, beauty. We call ourselves Christians, Buddhists, or Hindus and think we have solved the whole problem. We must shed all that, let it drop away completely, and it will drop away only when we begin to know ourselves deeply. It is only through understanding ourselves that we shall find something which is beyond all measure.

These are not mere words for you to learn and repeat. What you repeat will have no meaning unless you directly experience this. If you do not have your own direct understanding of it, the world of effort and sorrow, of misery and chaos, will continue.

Question: You talk so much against the church and organized religion. Have they not done a lot of good in this world?

KRISHNAMURTI: I am not talking against the church and organized religion. It is up to you. Personally I do not belong to any church or organized religion because to me, they have no meaning, and I think that if you are earnestly seeking what is real, you will have to put all those things aside—which does not mean that I am attacking. If you attack, you have to defend, but we are neither attacking nor defending. We are trying to understand this whole problem of existence, in which the church and organized religions are included.

I do not think any organized religion helps man to find God, truth. They may condition you to believe in God, as the communist mind is conditioned not to believe in God, but I do not see much difference between the two. The man who says, "I believe in God," and who has been trained from childhood to believe in God, is in the same field as the man who says, "I do not believe in God," and who has also been conditioned to repeat this kind of nonsense. But a man who wants to find out, begins to inquire for himself. He does not merely accept some authority, some book or savior. If he is really in earnest, pursuing understanding in his daily thoughts, in his whole way of life, he abandons all belief and disbelief. He is an inquirer, a real seeker, without any motive; he is on a journey of discovery, single, alone. And when he finds truth, life has quite a different significance. Then perhaps he may be able to help others to be free.

The questioner wants to know if the organized religions have not done good. Have they? I believe there is only one organized religion which has not brought misery to man through war—and it is obviously not Christianity. You have had more wars, perhaps, than any other religion—all in the name of peace, love, goodness, freedom. You have probably suffered more than most people the terrors of war and degradation—with both sides always claiming that God is with them. You know all this so well, without my repetition.

I think it is we who have made this world what it is. The world has not been made by wisdom, by truth, by God; we have made it, you and I. And until you and I fundamentally change, no organized religion is going to do good to man. They may socially do good, bring about superficial reforms. But it has taken centuries to civilize religions, and it will take centuries to civilize communism. A man who is really in earnest must be free from all these things. He must go beyond all the saviors, all the gods and demagogues, to find out what is true.

Question: Will self-knowledge put an end to suffering, which apparently necessitates the soul taking birth over and over again?

KRISHNAMURTI: The idea is that so long as you have to suffer, you must be reborn, until you transcend suffering. That is the old Hindu, Buddhist, or Asiatic idea. They say you must return to the earth, be reborn over and over again and continue to suffer until you understand the whole process of suffering and step out of it.

In one way it is true, is it not? Our life is suffering. Year after year, from the time we are born until we die, our life is a process of struggle, suffering, pain, anxiety, fear. We know this all too well. It is a form of continuity—the continuity of suffering, is it not? Whether you will be reborn, to suffer again until you understand, is irrelevant. You do suffer now, within the present lifetime. And can we put an end to suffering, not at some future date, but immediately, and not think in terms of time?

I think it is possible. Not that you must accept what I say because acceptance has no validity. But can one not begin to inquire for oneself whether suffering can come to an end? I am talking of psychological suffering, not the bodily aches and pains—although if we understand the psychological state of the mind, it may perhaps help to ameliorate our physical suffering also. So, can suffering come to an end? Or is man doomed to suffer everlastingly—not in the Christian sense of hellfire and all that rubbish, but in the ordinary sense? After all, fifty years or so of suffering is good enough. You don't have to speculate about the future.

If we begin to inquire into it, I think we shall find that suffering exists so long as there is ignorance of the whole process of one's own being. So long as I do not know myself, the ways and compulsions of my own mind, unconscious as well as conscious, there must be suffering. After all, we suffer because of ignorance—ignorance in the sense of not knowing oneself. Ignorance is also a lack of understanding of the ordinary daily contacts between man and man, and out of that ignorance comes much suffering also, but I am talking of our utter lack of self-knowledge. Without self-knowledge, suffering will continue.

Question: Is it possible to influence the thinking of mankind in the right direction by suitable thoughts and meditation?

KRISHNAMURTI: I think this is one of the most extraordinary concerns of man—the desire to influence somebody else. That is what you are all doing, is it not? You are trying to influence your son, your daughter, your husband, your wife, everybody around you—thinking that you know and the other does not. It is a form of vanity.

Really, what do you know? Very little, surely. You may be a great scientist and know a lot of facts; you may know many things that have been written in books, you may know about philosophy and psychology—but these are all merely the acquisitions of memory. And beyond that, what do you know? Yet you want to influence people in the right direction. That is what the communists are doing. They think they know; they interpret history in a certain way, as the church does, and they all want to influence people. And they jolly well are influencing people—putting them in concentration camps, trapping them with threats of hellfire, excommunication, and all the rest of it. You know all this business—which is supposed to be influencing people in the right direction. Those who do the influencing think they know what the right direction is. They all claim to have the vision of what is true. The communists claim it, and in the case of the church, it is supposed to be God-given. And you want to join one or the other of them, through "right thinking," as you call it.

But first of all, do you know what thinking is? Can there ever be right thinking so long as the mind is conditioned, so long as you are thinking of yourself as a Christian, a communist, or what you will? Surely the whole idea of trying to influence people is totally wrong.

Then you may ask, "What are you trying to do?" I assure you I am not trying to influence you. I am pointing out certain obvious things which perhaps you have not thought about before—and the rest is up to you. There is no "good" influence or "bad" influence when you are seeking what is true. To find out for oneself what is true, all influence must cease. There is no "good" conditioning or "bad" conditioning—there is only freedom from all conditioning. So the idea of trying to influence another for his "good" seems to me utterly immature, completely false.

Then there is this problem of meditation which the questioner raises. It is a very complex problem, and I do not know if you want to go into it.

Unless we know for ourselves what meditation is and how to meditate, life has very little depth. Without meditation, there is no perfume to life, no beauty, no love. Meditation is a tremendous thing, requiring a great deal of insight, perception. One may know that state, one may feel it occasionally. When one is sitting very quietly in one's room or under a tree looking at the blue sky, there comes a feeling of immensity without measure, without comparison, without cognition. But that is entirely different from the things that you have learned about meditation. You have probably read various books from India, telling how to meditate, and so you want to learn a technique in order to meditate.

The very process of learning a technique in which to meditate is a denial of meditation. Meditation is something entirely different. It is not the outcome of any practice, of any discipline, of any compulsion or conformity. But if you begin to understand the process of conformity, of compulsion, the desire to achieve, to gain something, then the understanding of all that is part of meditation. Self-knowledge—which is to know the ways of your own thought and to pursue thought right to the end—is the beginning of meditation.

It is very difficult to pursue a thought to the end because other thoughts come in, and then we say we must learn concentration. But concentration is not important. Any child is capable of concentration—give him a new toy and he is concentrated. Every businessman is concentrated when he wants to make money. Concentration, which we think we should have in order to meditate, is really narrowness, a process of limitation, exclusion.

So when you put the question, "How am I to meditate?" what is important is to understand why you ask "how." If you go into it, you will find this very inquiry is meditation.

But that is only a beginning. In meditation there is no thinker apart from thought; there is neither the pursuer nor the pursued. It is a state of being in which there is no sense of the experiencer. But to come to that state, the mind must really understand the whole process of itself. If it does not understand itself, it will get caught in its own projection, in a vision which it has created, and to be caught in a vision is not meditation.

Meditation is the process of understanding oneself; that is the beginning of it. Self-knowledge brings wisdom. And as the mind begins to understand the whole process of itself, it becomes very quiet, completely still, without any sense of movement or demand. Then, perhaps, that which is not measurable comes into being.

September 16, 1956

The Krishnamurti Foundations exist
to provide resources for the discovery, study,
and preservation of the work of J. Krishnamurti.

www.jkrishnamurti.org